BEGINNING SOLO Guitar

Disney Songs

T0077037

The following songs are the property of
Bourne Co.
Music Publishers
5 West 37th Street
New York, NY 10018

SOME DAY MY PRINCE WILL COME
WHEN YOU WISH UPON A STAR
WHISTLE WHILE YOU WORK

Disney Characters and Artwork © Disney

ISBN 978-1-4950-9761-4

7777 W. BLUEMOUND RD. P.O. BOX 13819 MILWAUKEE, WI 53213

Visit Hal Leonard Online at
www.halleonard.com

GUITAR NOTATION LEGEND

THE MUSICAL STAFF shows pitches and rhythms and is divided by bar lines into measures. Pitches are named after the first seven letters of the alphabet.

TABLATURE graphically represents the guitar fingerboard. Each horizontal line represents a string, and each number represents a fret.

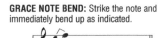

4th string, 2nd fret · 1st & 2nd strings open, played together · open D chord

HALF-STEP BEND: Strike the note and bend up 1/2 step.

WHOLE-STEP BEND: Strike the note and bend up one step.

GRACE NOTE BEND: Strike the note and immediately bend up as indicated.

SLIGHT (MICROTONE) BEND: Strike the note and bend up 1/4 step.

BEND AND RELEASE: Strike the note and bend up as indicated, then release back to the original note. Only the first note is struck.

PRE-BEND: Bend the note as indicated, then strike it.

VIBRATO: The string is vibrated by rapidly bending and releasing the note with the fretting hand.

PALM MUTING: The note is partially muted by the pick hand lightly touching the string(s) just before the bridge.

HAMMER-ON: Strike the first (lower) note with one finger, then sound the higher note (on the same string) with another finger by fretting it without picking.

PULL-OFF: Place both fingers on the notes to be sounded. Strike the first note and without picking, pull the finger off to sound the second (lower) note.

LEGATO SLIDE: Strike the first note and then slide the same fret-hand finger up or down to the second note. The second note is not struck.

SHIFT SLIDE: Same as legato slide, except the second note is struck.

TRILL: Very rapidly alternate between the notes indicated by continuously hammering on and pulling off.

TAPPING: Hammer ("tap") the fret indicated with the pick-hand index or middle finger and pull off to the note fretted by the fret hand.

NATURAL HARMONIC: Strike the note while the fret-hand lightly touches the string directly over the fret indicated.

Harm.

PINCH HARMONIC: The note is fretted normally and a harmonic is produced by adding the edge of the thumb or the tip of the index finger of the pick hand to the normal pick attack.

P.H.

TREMOLO PICKING: The note is picked as rapidly and continuously as possible.

VIBRATO BAR DIVE AND RETURN: The pitch of the note or chord is dropped a specified number of steps (in rhythm), then returned to the original pitch.

w/ bar

VIBRATO BAR SCOOP: Depress the bar just before striking the note, then quickly release the bar.

w/ bar

VIBRATO BAR DIP: Strike the note and then immediately drop a specified number of steps, then release back to the original pitch.

w/ bar

Additional Musical Definitions

(accent) · Accentuate note (play it louder).

(staccato) · Play the note short.

D.S. al Coda · Go back to the sign (𝄋), then play until the measure marked "*To Coda*," then skip to the section labelled "**Coda**."

D.C. al Fine · Go back to the beginning of the song and play until the measure marked "*Fine*" (end).

Fill · Label used to identify a brief melodic figure which is to be inserted into the arrangement.

N.C. · Harmony is implied.

· Repeat measures between signs.

· When a repeated section has different endings, play the first ending only the first time and the second ending only the second time.

The Bare Necessities

from THE JUNGLE BOOK

Words and Music by Terry Gilkyson

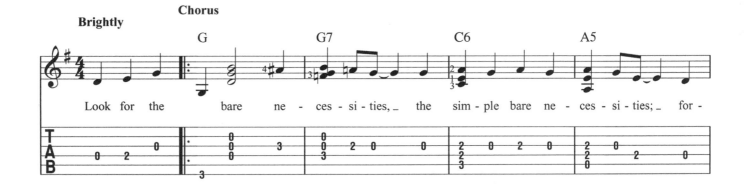

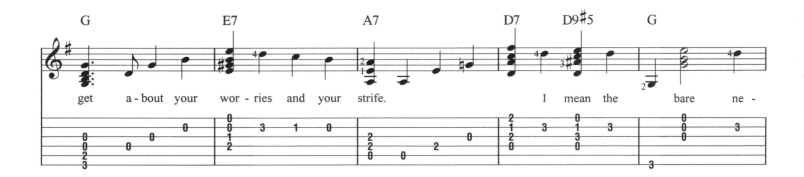

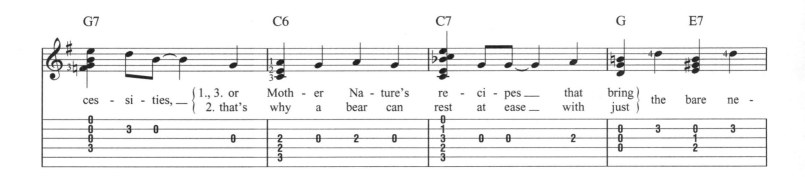

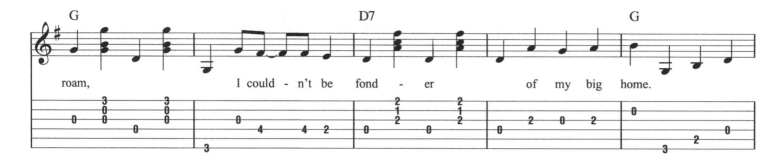

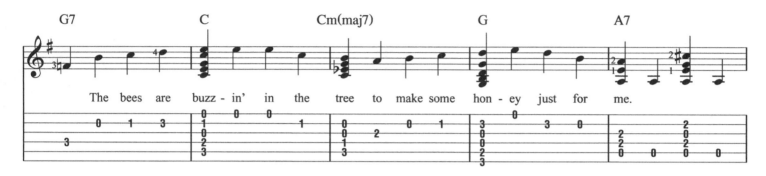

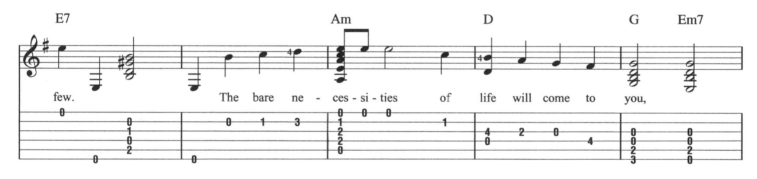

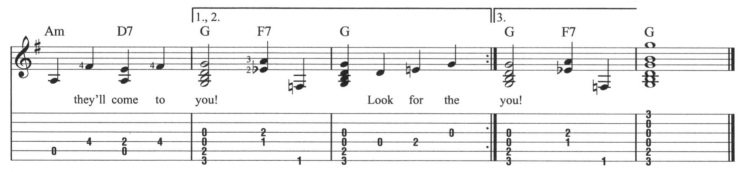

Additional Lyrics

2. When you pick a paw-paw or prickly pear,
And you prick a raw paw next time beware.
Don't pick the prickly pear by paw.
When you pick a pear, try to use the claw.
But you don't need to use the claw
When you pick a pear of the big paw-paw.
Have I given you a clue?
The bare necessities of life will come to you,
They'll come to you!

3. So just try to relax (Oh, yeah!) in my back yard,
If you act like the bee acts you're workin' too hard.
Don't spend your time just lookin' around
For something you want that can't be found.
When you find out you can live without it
And go along not thinkin' about it.
I'll tell you something true:
The bare necessities of life will come to you,
They'll come to you!

Beauty and the Beast

from BEAUTY AND THE BEAST

Music by Alan Menken
Lyrics by Howard Ashman

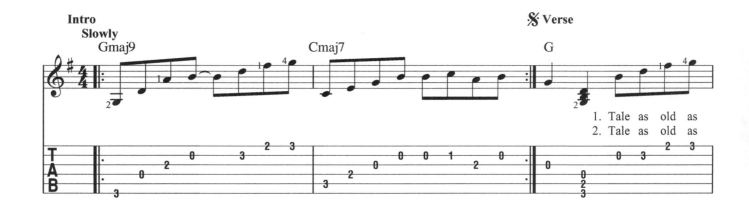

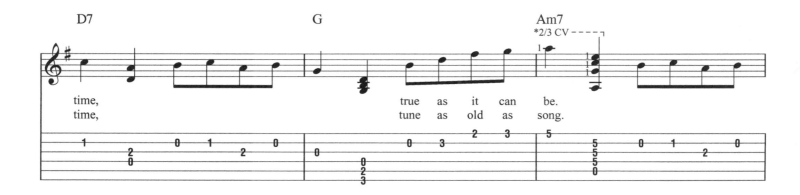

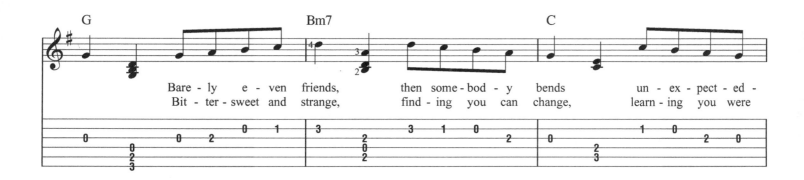

*"C" denotes barre. Fractional prefix indicates which strings are barred (e.g. 1/2 = first 3 strings.) Roman numeral suffix indicates barred fret.

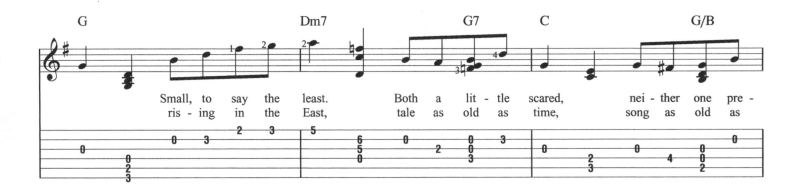

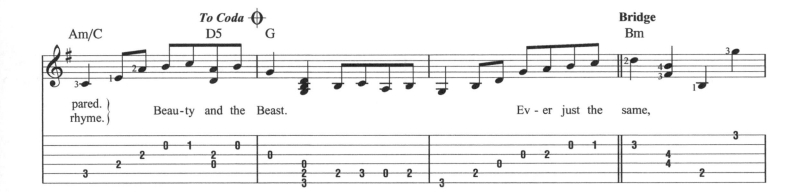

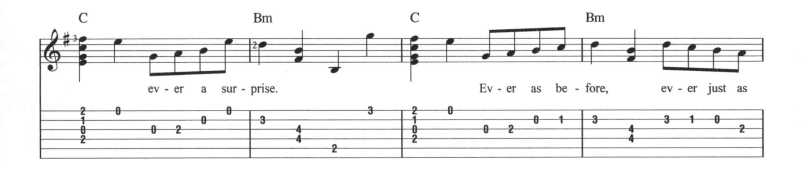

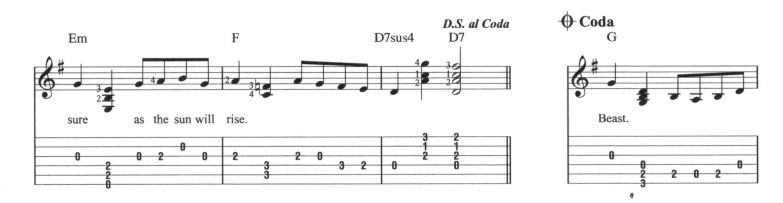

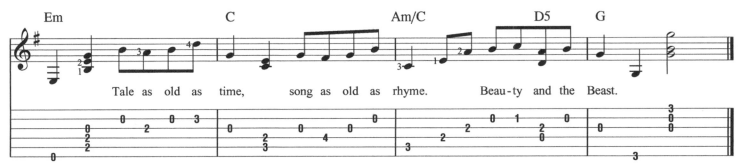

Can You Feel the Love Tonight

from THE LION KING

Music by Elton John
Lyrics by Tim Rice

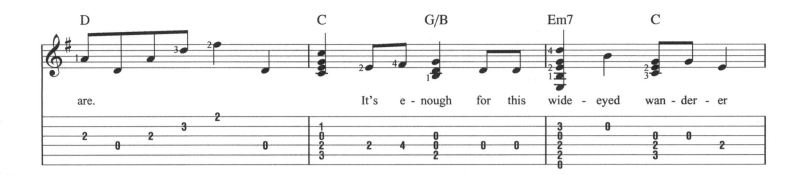

are. It's e-nough for this wide - eyed wan - der - er

that we got this far. And can you feel the love _

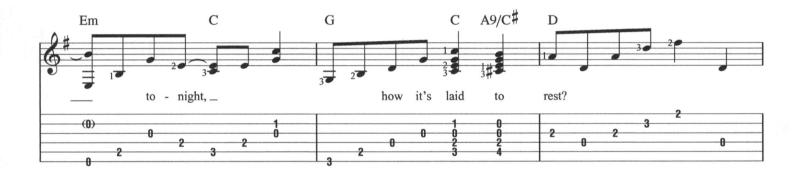

to - night, _ how it's laid to rest?

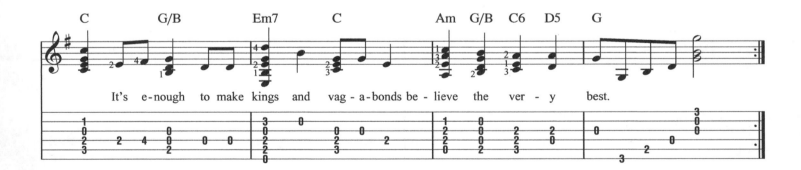

It's e-nough to make kings and vag - a-bonds be - lieve the ver - y best.

Outro

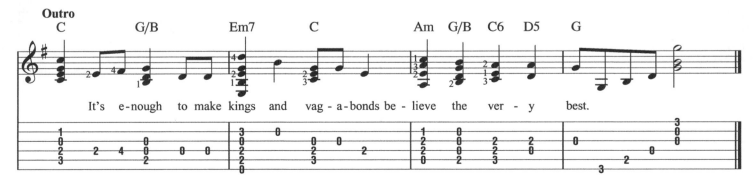

It's e-nough to make kings and vag - a-bonds be - lieve the ver - y best.

Chim Chim Cher-ee

from MARY POPPINS

Words and Music by Richard M. Sherman and Robert B. Sherman

Chorus
Fast

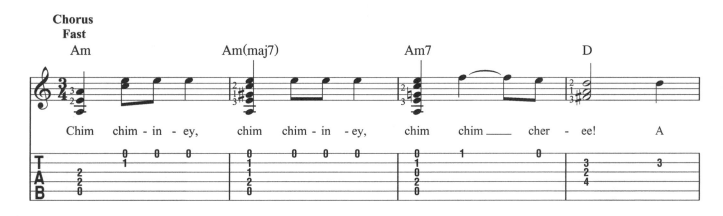

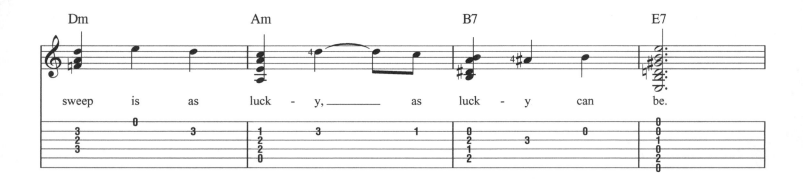

Chim chim - in - ey, chim chim - in - ey, chim chim ___ cher - ee! A

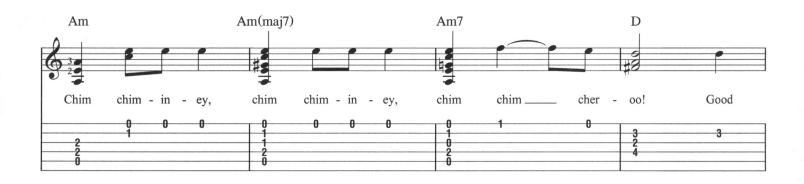

sweep is as luck - y, ___ as luck - y can be.

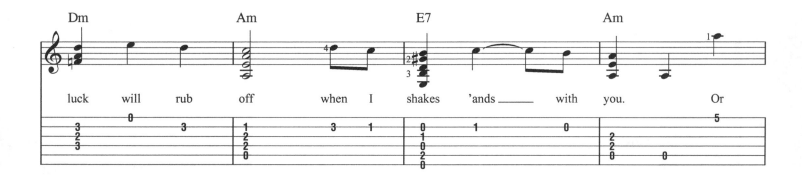

Chim chim - in - ey, chim chim - in - ey, chim chim ___ cher - oo! Good

luck will rub off when I shakes 'ands ___ with you. Or

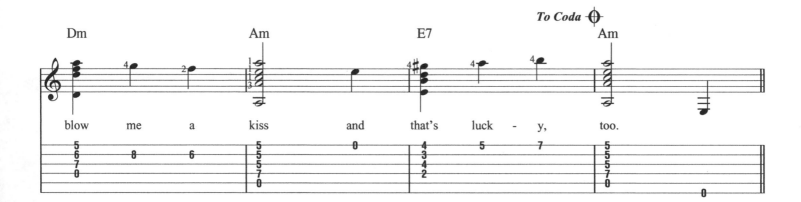

To Coda ⊕

| Dm | Am | E7 | Am |

blow me a kiss and that's luck - y, too.

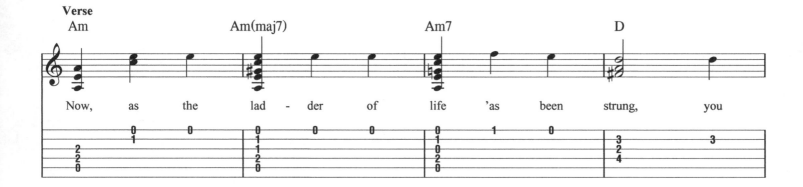

Verse

| Am | Am(maj7) | Am7 | D |

Now, as the lad - der of life 'as been strung, you

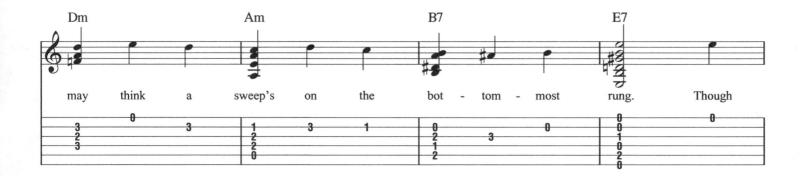

| Dm | Am | B7 | E7 |

may think a sweep's on the bot - tom - most rung. Though

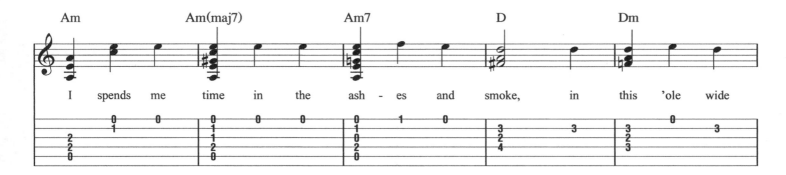

| Am | Am(maj7) | Am7 | D | Dm |

I spends me time in the ash - es and smoke, in this 'ole wide

D.C. al Coda   ⊕ **Coda**

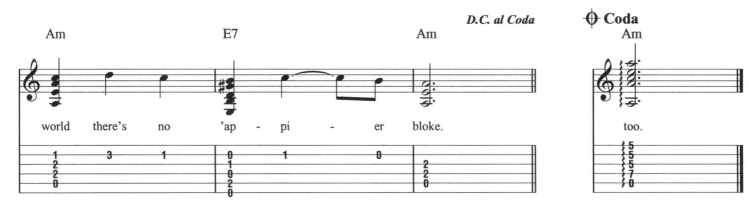

| Am | E7 | Am | Am |

world there's no 'ap - pi - er bloke.   too.

A Dream Is a Wish Your Heart Makes

from CINDERELLA

Words and Music by Mack David, Al Hoffman and Jerry Livingston

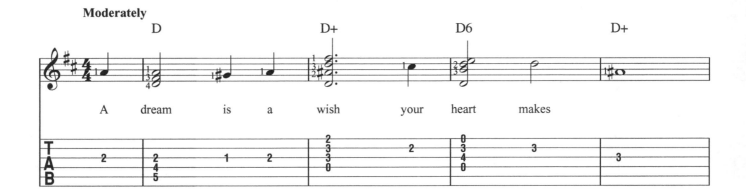

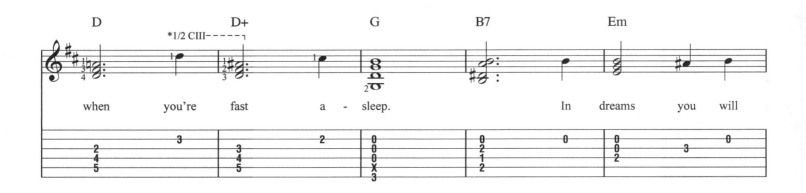

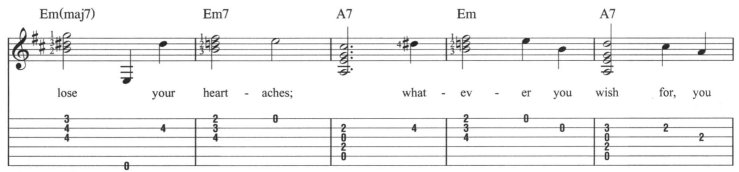

*"C" denotes brre. Fractional prefix indicates which strings are barred (e.g. 1/2 = first 3 strings). Roman numeral suffix indicates barred fret.

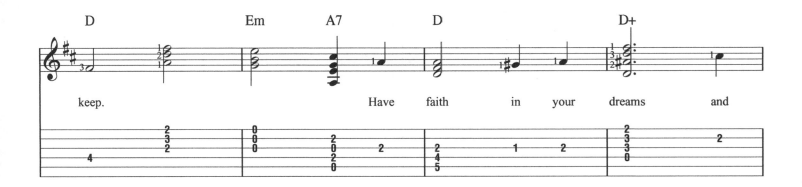

keep.   Have faith in your dreams and

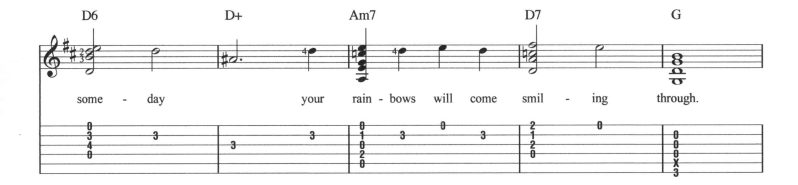

some - day   your rain - bows will come smil - ing through.

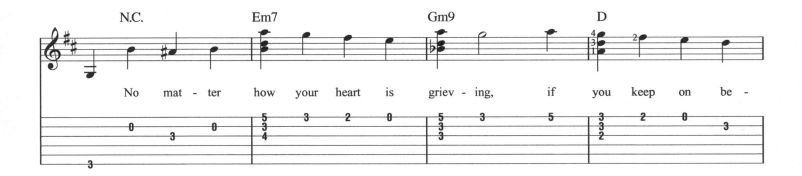

No mat - ter how your heart is griev - ing, if you keep on be -

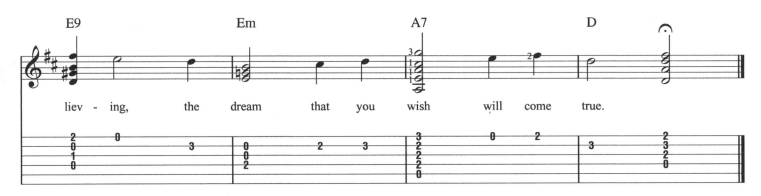

liev - ing, the dream that you wish will come true.

It's a Small World

from Disney Parks' "it's a small world" attraction

Words and Music by Richard M. Sherman and Robert B. Sherman

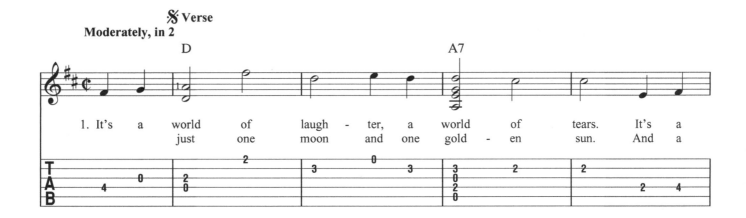

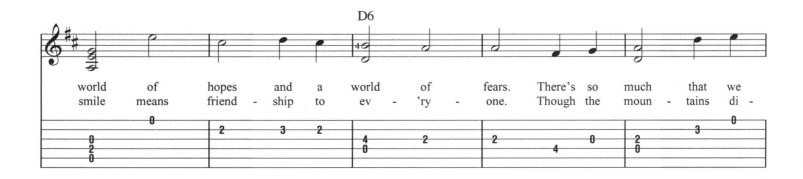

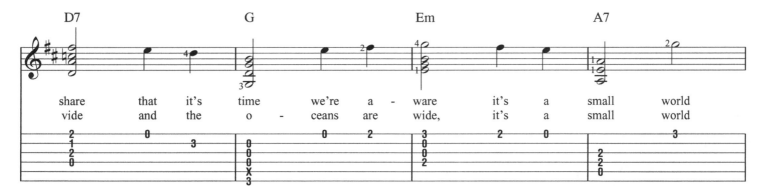

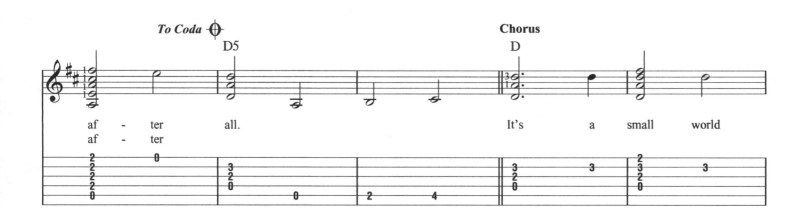

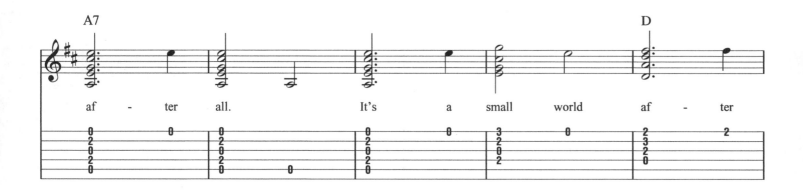

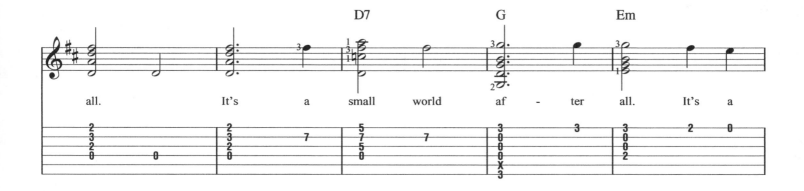

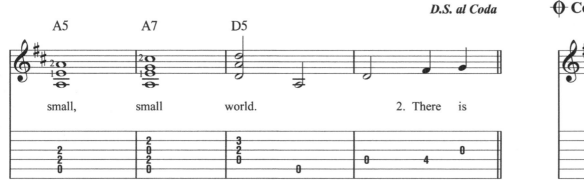

Part of Your World

from THE LITTLE MERMAID

Music by Alan Menken
Lyrics by Howard Ashman

Look at this stuff. _ Is - n't it neat? _ Would-n't you think _ my col - lect-ion's com - plete?

Would-n't you think _ I'm the girl, ___ the girl who has ev - 'ry - thing? _____

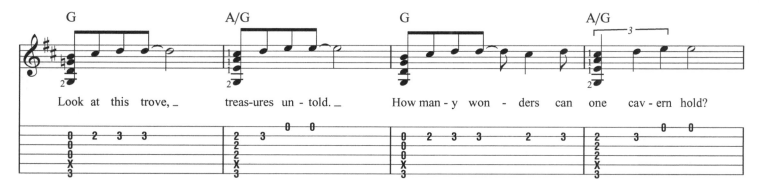

Look at this trove, _ treas-ures un - told. _ How man - y won - ders can one cav - ern hold?

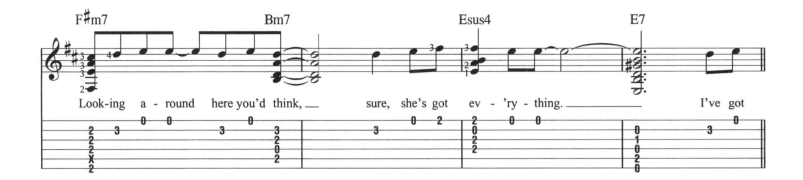

Look-ing a - round here you'd think, ___ sure, she's got ev - 'ry - thing. ___ I've got

Pre-Chorus

gad - gets and giz - mos a - plen-ty. ___ I've got who - zits and what - zits ga - lore. You want

thing-a - ma-bobs, I've got twen - ty. ___ But who cares? No big deal. I want

Chorus

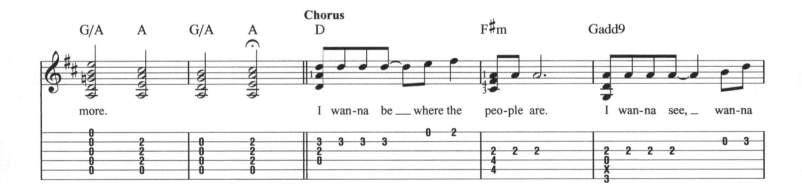

more. I wan-na be ___ where the peo-ple are. I wan-na see, ___ wan-na

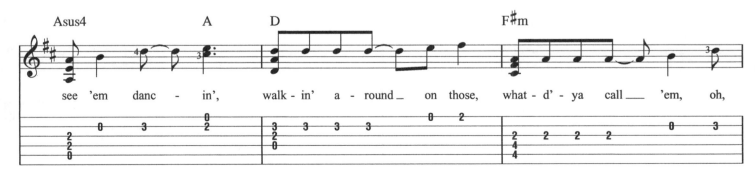

see 'em danc - in', walk - in' a - round ___ on those, what - d' - ya call ___ 'em, oh,

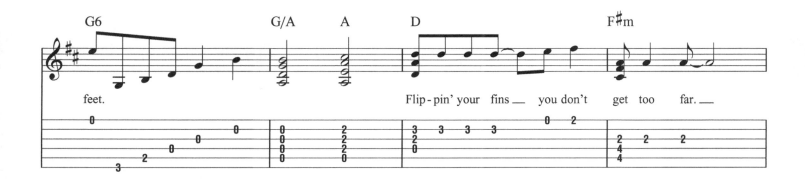

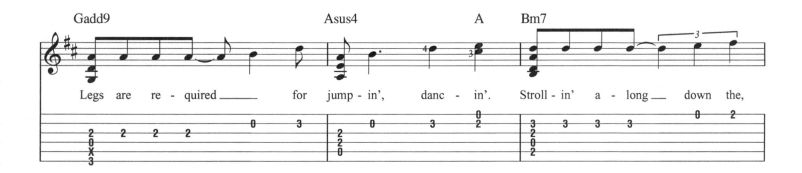

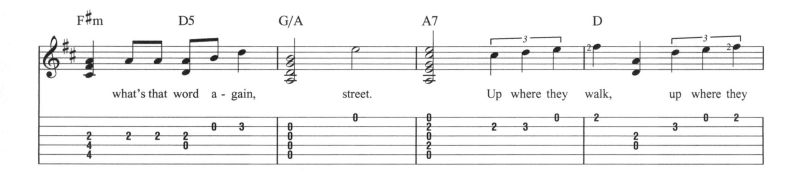

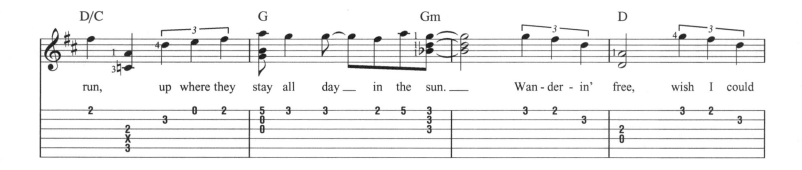

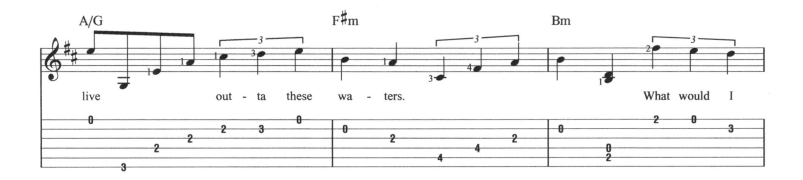

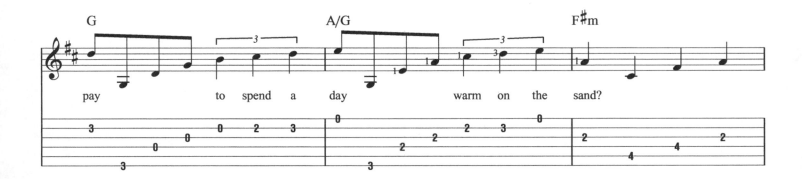

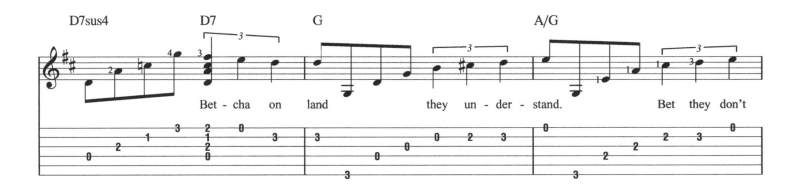

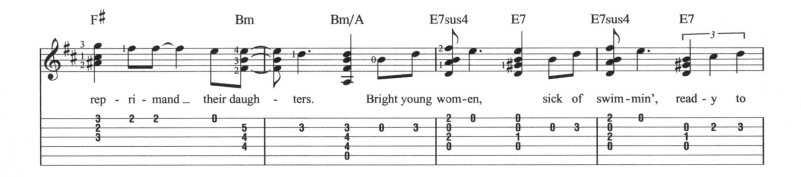

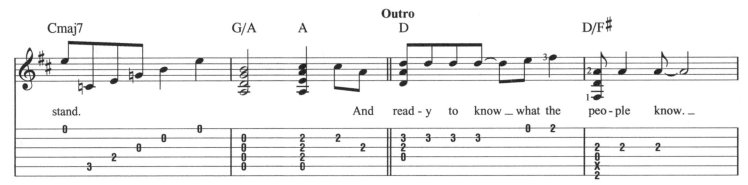

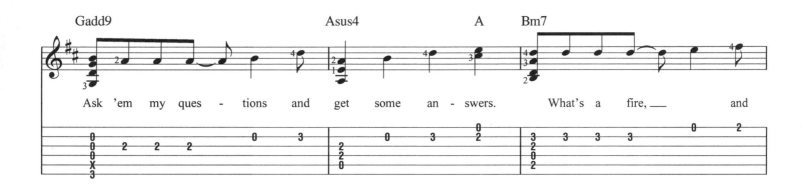

Ask 'em my ques - tions and get some an - swers. What's a fire, ___ and

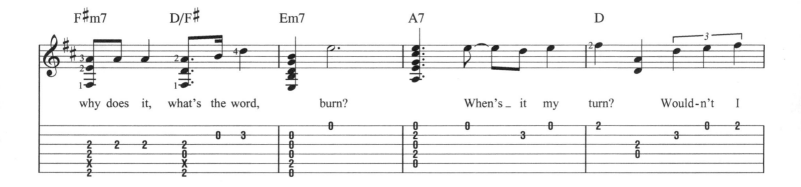

why does it, what's the word, burn? When's it my turn? Would-n't I

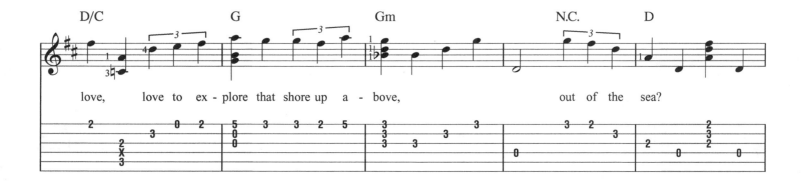

love, love to ex - plore that shore up a - bove, out of the sea?

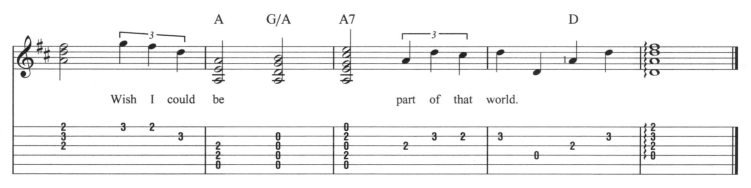

Wish I could be part of that world.

When You Wish Upon a Star

from PINOCCHIO

Words by Ned Washington
Music by Leigh Harline

Some Day My Prince Will Come

from SNOW WHITE AND THE SEVEN DWARFS

Words by Larry Morey
Music by Frank Churchill

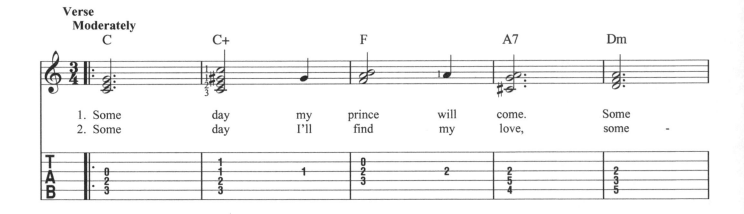

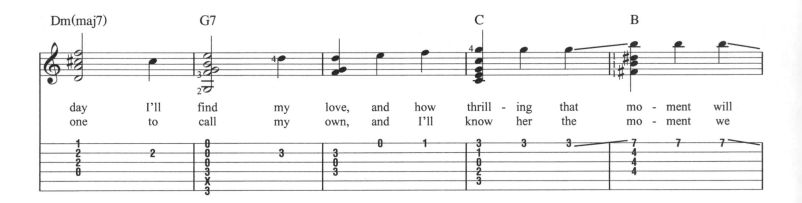

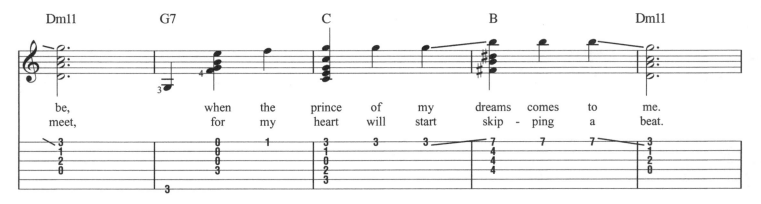

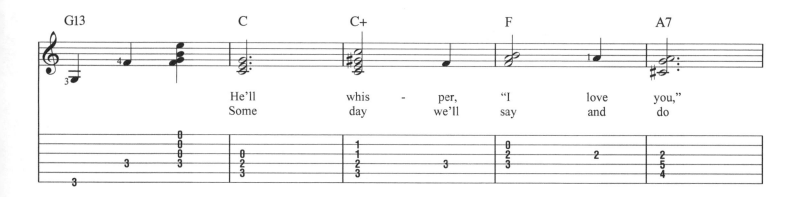

He'll   whis - per,   "I   love   you,"
Some   day   we'll   say   love   and   do

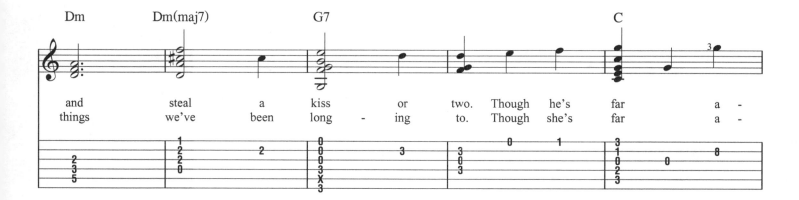

and   steal   a   kiss   or   two. Though   he's   far   a -
things   we've   been   long - ing   to. Though   she's   far   a -

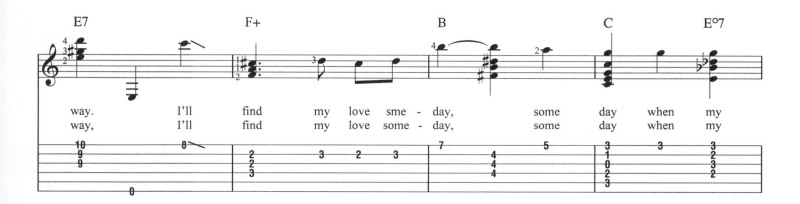

way.   I'll   find   my   love   sme - day,   some   day   when   my
way,   I'll   find   my   love   some - day,   some   day   when   my

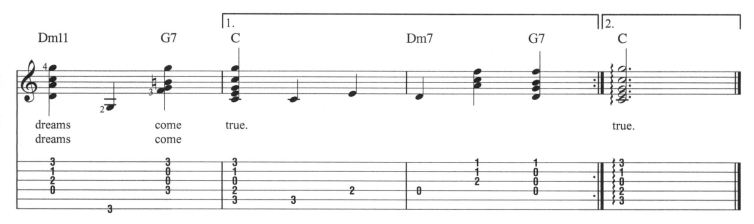

dreams   come   true.
dreams   come   come   true.

When She Loved Me

from TOY STORY 2
Music and Lyrics by Randy Newman

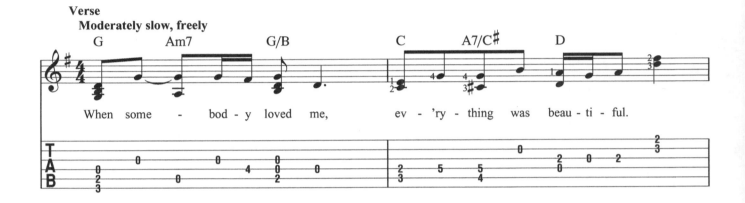

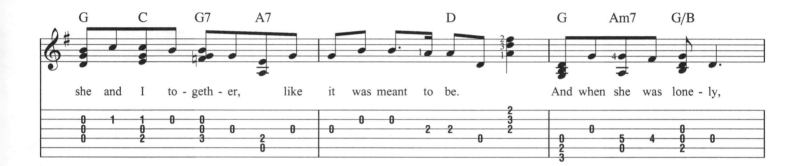

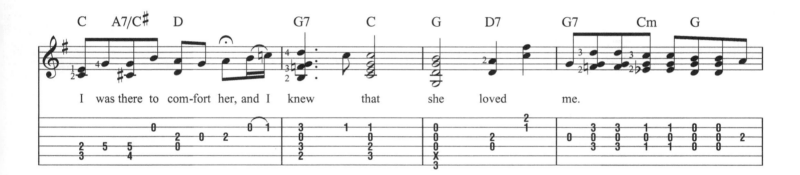

Bridge

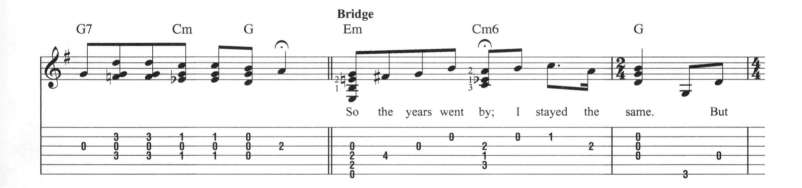

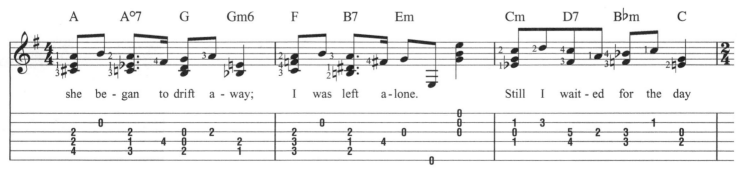

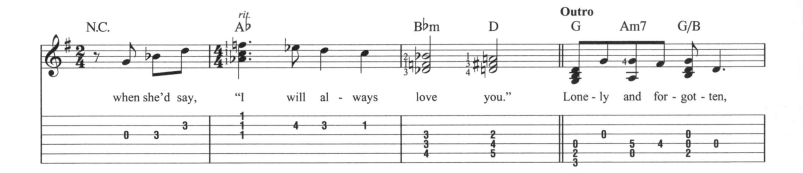

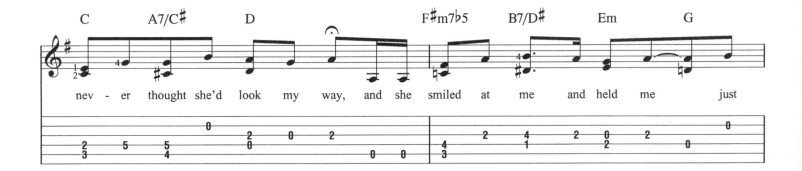

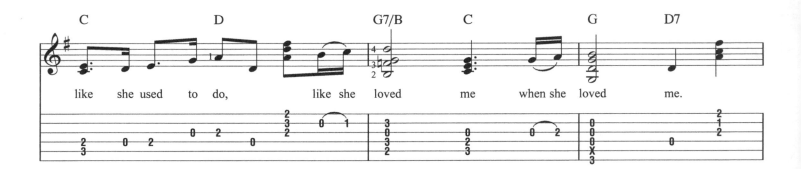

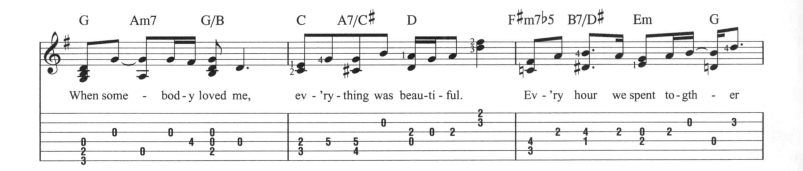

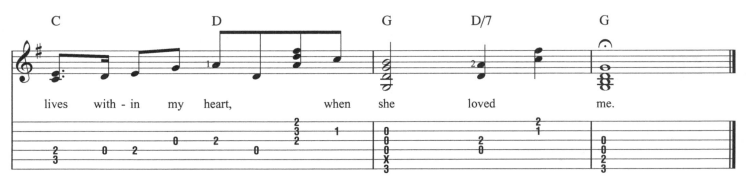

Whistle While You Work

from SNOW WHITE AND THE SEVEN DWARFS

Words by Larry Morey
Music by Frank Churchill

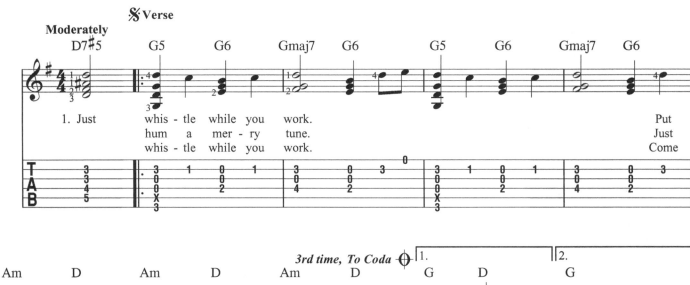

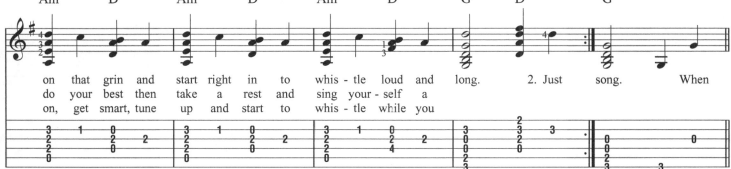

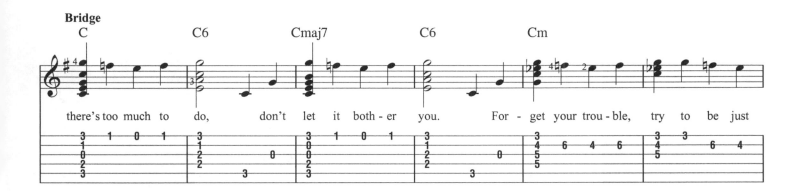

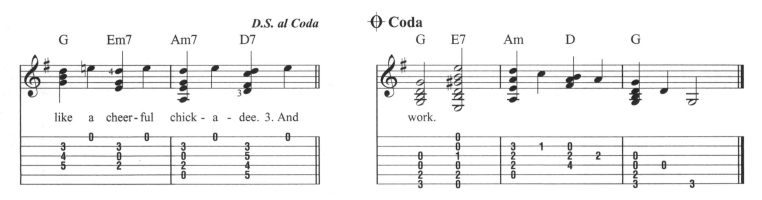

Written in the Stars

from AIDA

Music by Elton John
Lyrics by Tim Rice

Intro
Moderately slow, in 2

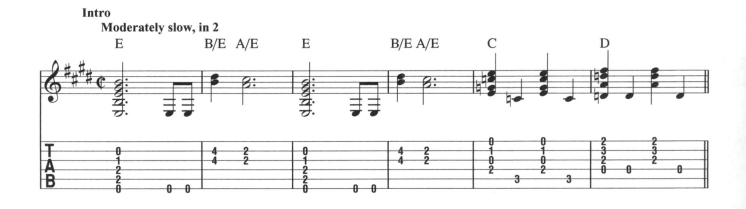

1. I am here to tell ____ you we can nev-er meet a-gain.
2., 3. *See additional lyrics*

Sim-ple real-ly, is-n't it? A word or two and then ____ a

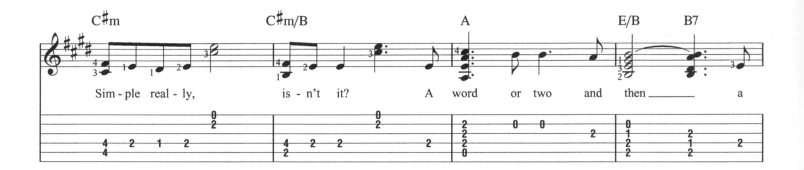

life-time of not know-ing where or how or why or when. You

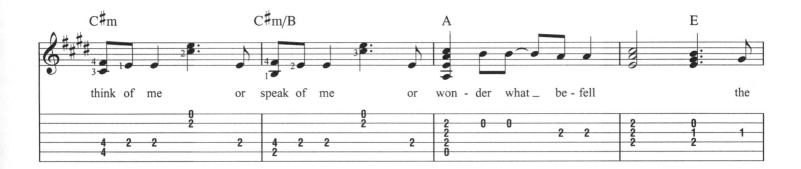

think of me   or speak of me   or won - der what __ be - fell   the

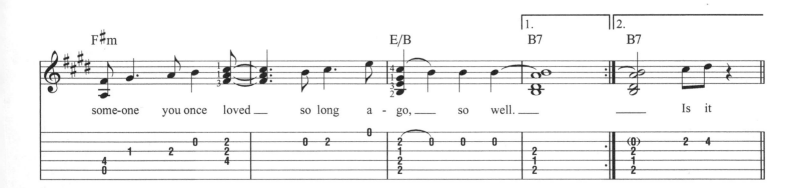

some-one you once loved __   so long   a - go, __ so   well. __   __   Is it

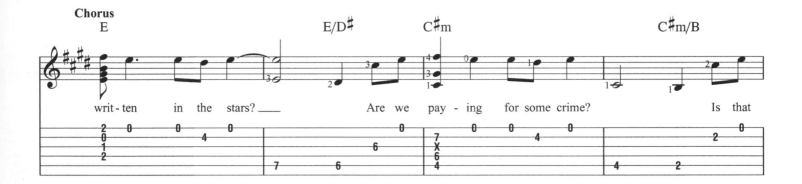

Chorus

writ - ten   in   the stars? __   Are we   pay - ing   for some crime?   Is that

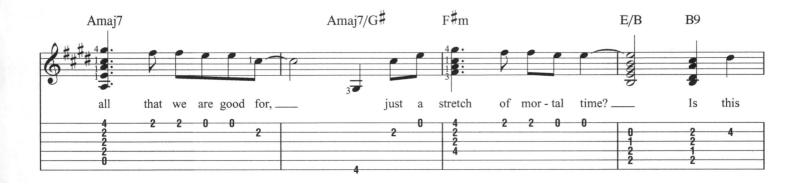

all   that we are good for, __   just a stretch of mor - tal time? __   Is this

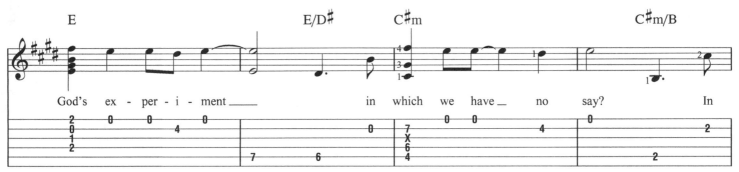

God's ex - per - i - ment __   in which we have __ no say?   In

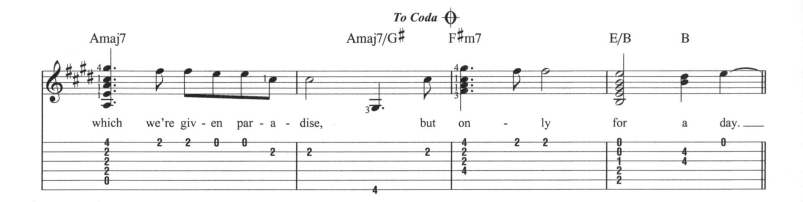

To Coda ⊕

which we're giv-en par-a-dise, but on-ly for a day.____

D.S. al Coda
(take 2nd ending)

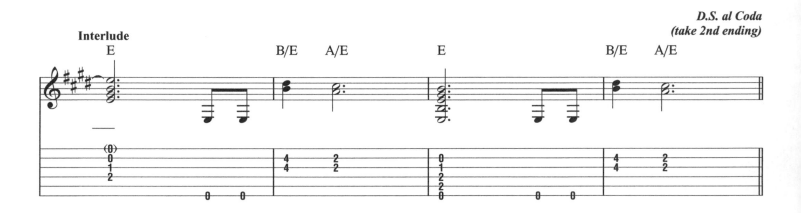

Interlude

⊕ **Coda**

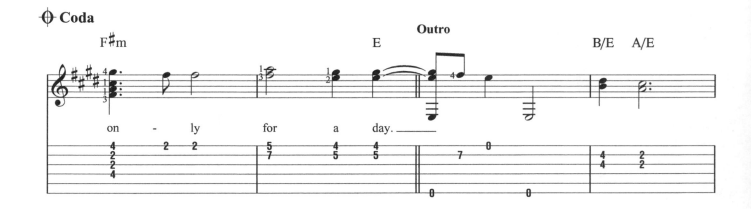

Outro

on-ly for a day.____

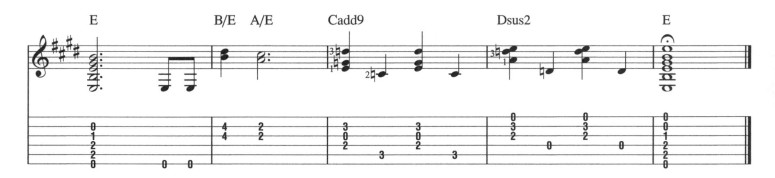

Additional Lyrics

2. Never wonder what I'll feel as living shuffles by.
You don't have to ask me, and I need not reply.
Every moment of my life from now until I die,
I will think or dream of you and fail to understand
How a perfect love can be confounded out of hand.

3. Nothing can be altered. Oh, there is nothing to decide.
No excape, no change of heart, nor any place to hide.
You are all I'll ever want, but this I am denied.
Sometimes in my darkest thoughts I wish I never learned
What it is to be in love and have that love returned.

You've Got a Friend in Me

from TOY STORY

Music and Lyrics by Randy Newman

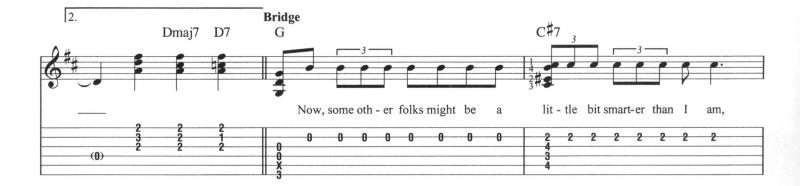

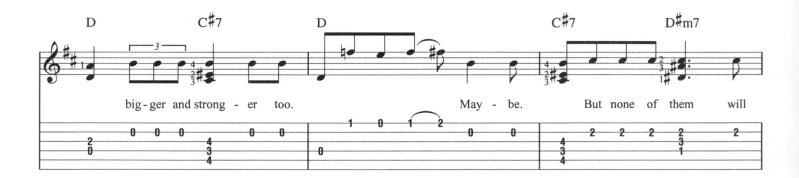

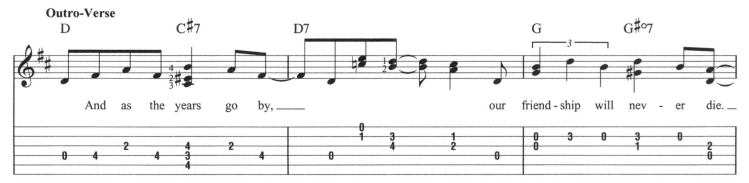

*w/ pick and fingers

You're gon - na   see   it's our   des - ti - ny.

You've got a friend in   me. ____   You've got   a   friend in   me. ____

Yeah, you've ____ got   a friend in me.

Additional Lyrics

2. You've got a friend in me.
   You've got a friend in me.
   You got troubles, then I got 'em too.
   There isn't anything I wouldn't do for you.
   If we stick together we can see it through,
   'Cause you've got a friend in me.
   Yeah, you've got a friend in me.

You'll Be in My Heart*

from TARZAN™

Words and Music by Phil Collins

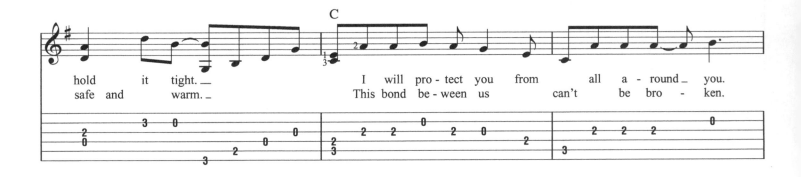

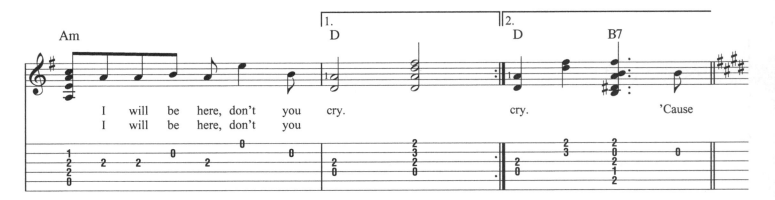

Chorus

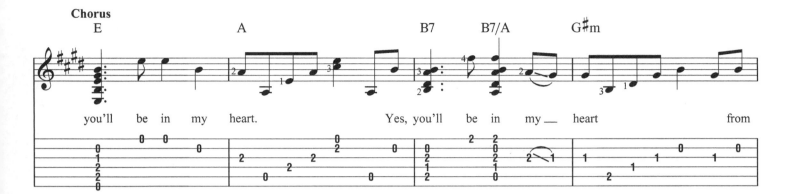

you'll be in my heart. Yes, you'll be in my ___ heart from

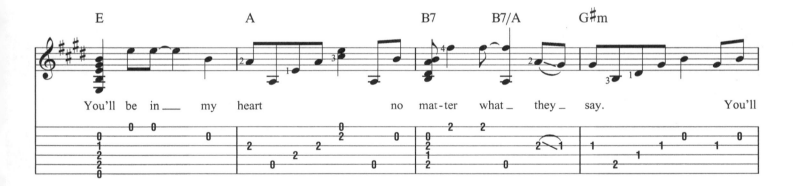

this day on, ___ now and ___ for - ev - er - more. ___

You'll be in ___ my heart no mat - ter what ___ they ___ say. You'll

be here in ___ my heart al - ways.

Zip-A-Dee-Doo-Dah

from SONG OF THE SOUTH

Words by Ray Gilbert
Music by Allie Wrubel

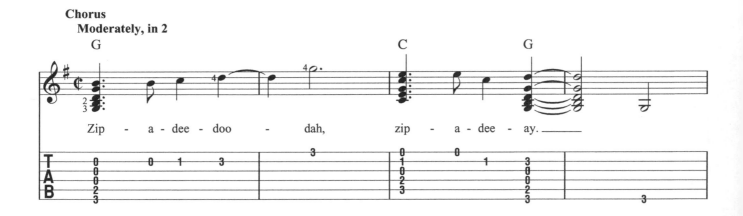

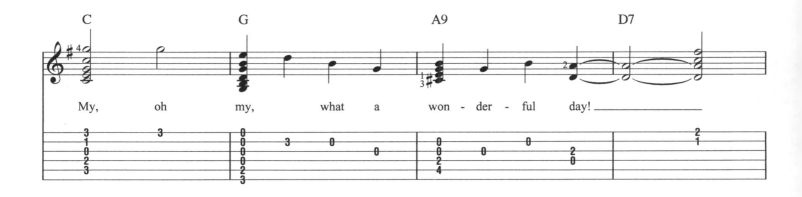

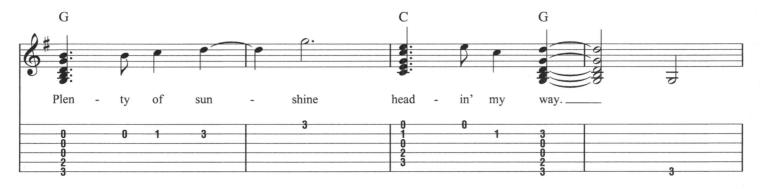

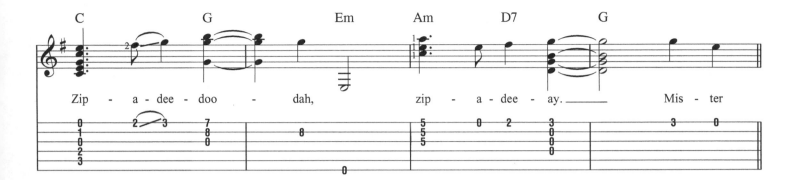

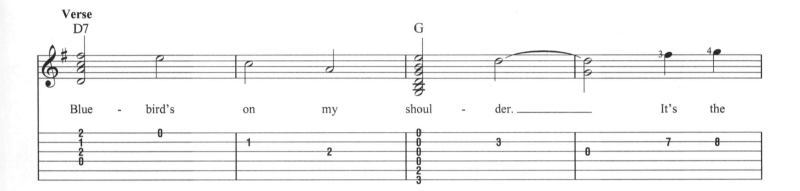

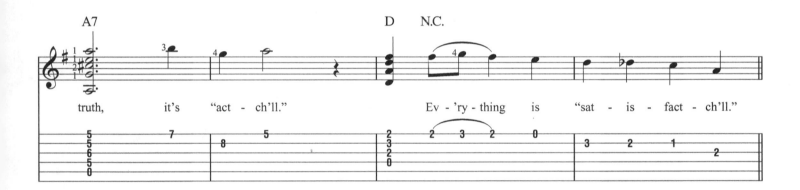

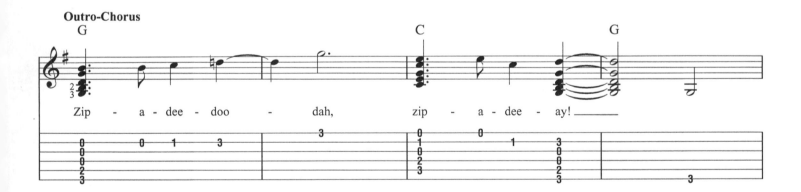

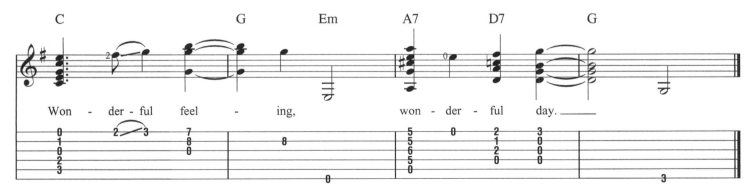